D0649065

& My Brothers

Volume 4

Hari Tokeino

Me & My Brothers Volume 4

Created by Hari Tokeino

Translation - Haruko Furukawa
English Adaptation - Jeffrey Reeves
Copy Editor - Shannon Watters
Retouch and Lettering - Star Print Brokers
Production Artist - Keila N. Ramos
Graphic Designer - Mona Lisa de Asis

Editor - Hyun Joo Kim
Digital Imaging Manager - Chris Buford
Pre-Production Supervisor - Lucas Rivera
Production Manager - Elisabeth Brizzi
Managing Editor - Vy Nguyen
Creative Director - Anne Marie Horne
Editor-in-Chief - Rob Tokar
Publisher - Mike Kiley
President and C.O.O. - John Parker
C.E.O. and Chief Creative Officer - Stu Levy

A TOKYOPOP® Manga

TOKYOPOP and are trademarks or registered trademarks of TOKYOPOP Inc.

TOKYOPOP Inc.
5900 Wilshire Blvd. Suite 2000
Los Angeles, CA 90036

E-mail: info@TOKYOPOP.com
Come visit us online at www.TOKYOPOP.com

ONIICHAN TO ISSHO by Hari Tokeino © 2004 Hari Tokeino All rights reserved. First published in Japan in 2005 by HAKUSENSHA, INC., Tokyo English language translation rights in the United States of America and Canada arranged with HAKUSENSHA, INC., Tokyo through Tuttle-Mori Agency Inc., Tokyo
English text copyright © 2008 TOKYOPOP Inc.

All rights reserved. No portion of this book may be reproduced or transmitted in any form or by any means without written permission from the copyright holders. This manga is a work of fiction. Any resemblance to actual events or locales or persons, living or dead, is entirely coincidental.

ISBN: 978-1-4278-0074-9

First TOKYOPOP printing: June 2008

10 9 8 7 6 5 4 3 2 1

Printed in the USA

Me & My Brothers

Volume 4

Hari Tokeino

TOKYOPOP®

HAMBURG // LONDON // LOS ANGELES // TOKYO

Contents

EPISODE 15.....3

EPISODE 16.....35

EPISODE 17.....65

EPISODE 18.....97

EPISODE 19.....127

HOW TO GO THROUGH THE SECRET DOOR.....159

BONUS PAGE.....191

Me & My Brothers

Episode 15

CHARACTERS PROFILE

ME & MY BROTHERS

SAKURA MIYASHITA: THE YOUNGEST. IN 8TH GRADE. THE ONLY GIRL IN THE MIYASHITA FAMILY. SHE IS NOT BLOOD RELATED TO HER FOUR BROTHERS.

MASASHI MIYASHITA: THE ELDEST. ROMANCE NOVELIST. ACCORDING TO HIM, HE SOUNDS LIKE A WOMAN BECAUSE OF HIS JOB. HE'S THE LEADER OF THE FOUR SAKURA-SPOILERS.

TAKASHI MIYASHITA: THE 2ND BROTHER. TEACHER. HE TEACHES JAPANESE AT SAKURA'S SCHOOL. HE'S A GENTLEMAN.

TSUYOSHI MIYASHITA: THE 3RD BROTHER. FULL-TIME PART-TIMER. HE HAS A DIRTY MOUTH BUT IS ACTUALLY SHY.

TAKESHI MIYASHITA: THE 4TH BROTHER. IN 11TH GRADE. HE LOOKS OLD, BUT HE'S THE YOUNGEST OF FOUR BROTHERS. HE'S QUIET AND LOVES PLANTS.

NAKA-CHAN: SAKURA'S BEST FRIEND. HER FAMILY NAME IS TANAKA. A CHEERFUL GIRL.

SUZUKI-KUN: SAKURA'S CLASSMATE. DOES HE HAVE A CRUSH ON SAKURA?

STORY

SAKURA LOST HER PARENTS WHEN SHE WAS 3 AND WAS RAISED BY HER GRANDMOTHER. THEN, WHEN SAKURA TURNED 14, HER GRANDMOTHER PASSED AWAY. SHE WAS ALL ALONE UNTIL FOUR STEPBROTHERS SHOWED UP! THE STEPBROTHERS ARE FROM SAKURA'S FATHER'S FIRST MARRIAGE. WHILE HER STEPBROTHERS' FATHER HAD RAISED SAKURA AS HIS OWN, SAKURA'S BIRTH FATHER IS ACTUALLY HER MOTHER'S EX-BOYFRIEND. EVEN THOUGH THE BROTHERS HAVE NO BLOOD CONNECTION TO SAKURA, AFTER 11 YEARS OF SEPARATION, THEY STARTED TO LIVE TOGETHER! NOW THEIR HOUSE IS LIVELY EVERYDAY...

PLEASE READ *ME & MY BROTHERS* VOLUME 1-3 FOR MORE DETAILS!

THIS IS ALREADY THE SECOND NEW YEAR'S HOLIDAY...
CLAP
CLAP
TIME FLIES...
...THAT I'VE SPENT WITH MY BROTHERS.
PLEASE LET MY FAMILY BE WELL AND HAPPY.
And please let me pass my high school entrance exam.
I hate drawing cars. It's difficult.

MOTHER: FUMIKO OTSUKA ↓
...SHE FELL IN LOVE AND MARRIED DAD, WHO WAS LIVING WITH MY SOON-TO-BE BROTHERS AFTER HE LOST HIS WIFE.
15 YEARS AGO, WHEN MOM WAS PREGNANT WITH ME (HER EX-BOYFRIEND WAS MY BIRTH FATHER)...
You're finally finding out their full names after all this time.
FATHER: SHUNSUKE MIYASHITA↑
SEPARATED
AFTER THAT, I LIVED ALONE WITH MY GRANDMOTHER FOR A LONG TIME...
BUT BOTH MOM AND DAD BECAME STARS IN THE SKY WHEN I WAS THREE.
....INSTEAD, I WENT TO LIVE WITH MY BROTHERS... NOW I'M NEVER ALONE.
WHEN MY GRANDMOTHER PASSED AWAY...
...I THOUGHT I'D BE COMPLETELY ALONE, BUT...
WELL THEN! SHALL WE HOLD HANDS AND GO HOME, SAKURA-CHAN? ♥

NO THANKS.
"Hold hands"?
WHY NOT?! IT'S MY BIRTHDAY! LET ME DO WHAT I WANT TO DO!!
YOU'RE SO TINY! YOU'LL GET LOST IN THIS CROWD!
Masashi...
YOUR BIRTHDAY WAS YESTERDAY. WE ALREADY CELEBRATED IT.
Idiot.
THAT DOESN'T MEAN I'LL HOLD YOUR HAND!
YOU'LL BE ALL RIGHT IF YOU STAY IN THE MIDDLE OF US.
Right, Sakura-san?
Yeah, we'll shove everybody out of the way for ya.
HEY, WHERE DID TAKESHI GO?
.....
It's open today.
THERE'S THE CAFÉ WHERE MY FRIEND WORKS...
Friend?
Umeda-kun.
HOW CAN YOU BE SWEPT UP BY THE CROWD WHEN YOU'RE SO TALL?!
SHALL WE GO TO A CAFÉ AND TAKE A BREAK?
BONK
Tsu-yoshi...
SURE, BUT DO YOU KNOW OF ANY THAT ARE OPEN TODAY?

Nice place.
So cold.
DING
DONG
BYE-BYE...
GIVE ME YOUR ANSWER BY NEXT WEEK, OKAY?
Bon giorno!
WELCOME--
Tee hee!
DING
DONG
GASP
?
Let me go!
!

SIGNORINA!!
?!
Who, me?!
I CAN'T BELIEVE IT...
YOU LOOK EXACTLY LIKE MY LOVE, WHO'S PASSED AWAY...

ボカバキドガ
POP
...GIRLFRI--
PLEASE! BE MY...
UME-CHAN.
If you keep saying things like that to them, somebody will really come kill you.
WILL YOU STOP USING THAT PICK-UP LINE ON OUR CUSTOMERS, BOSS?
Ouch.
Oh, that's right, even death won't cure your stupidity.
Oh.
IS SHE YOUR FRIEND? INTRODUCE ME.
SAKURA
HAPPY
かっちり
By the way...
I SEE YOUR BROTHERS ARE OVER-PROTECTIVE, AS USUAL.
It wasn't a compliment.
KNOCKED OUT

カッ
I'M TAIZO FUKASAWA, 36 YEARS OLD, SINGLE... PLEASURE TO MEET YOU.
Signorina.
SHOVE

MASASHI MIYASHITA, 27, SINGLE. PLEASURE.
Thank you for your formal introduction.
SQUEEZE
.....

IF THAT'S HOW YOU SEE IT.
If he's calling you a pervert...
You pervert.
HUMPH!
ARE YOU CHALLENGING ME...
...BEAUTIFUL KNIGHT?

THEN ...
Where did they get the swords?
WHAT?!
WE DUEL!!
ENTHUSIASTIC
BRING IT ON.

ENOOOUGH!!
WHAT'RE YOU DOING?! THIS IS A COFFEE SHOP!! STOP IT RIGHT NOW!!
You're adults!! Don't you have any consideration for others?!
SCOLD
How sad.
15 years old
I don't care. The cafe is empty right now and he owns the place anyway.
36 years old
27 years old
UM, WE CAME HERE JUST TO REST, SO...
What's with this guy?
I used to be called "Master of Darts."
Okay!
NEXT, WE'LL COMPETE WITH DARTS!!
Humph.
THAT MAKES ME THE WINNER BY DEFAULT. NOW I CAN OFFICIALLY ASK HER OUT.
HUH?

PLEASE, GIVE ME A MOMENT!
Oops... Maybe I really will be killed.
I TAKE BACK WHAT I SAID!
I love you.
Oh, Taizo-san. I love you, too.
WHEN I WAS YOUNG, I HAD A GIRLFRIEND TO WHOM I SWORE MY ETERNAL LOVE AND DEVOTION.
Oh, my poor heart!
BEFORE YOU KILL ME, PLEASE HEAR MY TRAGIC LOVE STORY...
Wait for me, honey!!
BUT THE LOVERS WERE SEPARATED, FOR I HAD TO LEAVE TO BECOME THE ULTIMATE BARISTA!

You clean it up, okay?
ガッシャン
What's with the spotlight?
BUT WHEN I RETURNED...
...SHE WAS GONE... FOREVER.
TEARS
YOU REALLY DO LOOK JUST LIKE HER.
I'M THROWING A SMALL NEW YEAR'S PARTY AND I'VE INVITED MY CLIENTS AND FRIENDS.
I'D LIKE YOU TO COME, TOO.
I WANT YOU TO SEE HOW WELL I'VE DONE... FOR HER.

NO FREAKING WAY, FREAK!!
Are you kidding me?! You're way too old for her!!
L-lover?
Hide Sakura-chan! Quick!
SO YOU'LL COME WITH ME AS MY LOVER, WON'T YOU?
...LIKE PROFESSOR HIGGINS AND ELIZA DOOLITTLE, AGE DOESN'T MATTER.
AND...
IT'S ONLY FOR A DAY.
SHE'S SHORTER THAN THE 6TH GRADERS IN OUR NEIGHBORHOOD!
I absolutely must protest !!!
IT DOES MATTER !!!
Masashi...
You've gone too far.
Hey.
SHE'S STILL SO CUTE, SHE'D LOOK GOOD WITH AN ELEMENTARY SCHOOL BACKPACK!!
EVEN IF IT'S JUST FOR A DAY, SAKURA-CHAN IS TOO YOUNG FOR YOU TO LABEL HER YOUR "LOVER"!

Learn from your experiences, Masashi.
?!
Grazie!!
Thanks!!
I'D LOVE TO GO TO THE PARTY WITH YOU.
Sissy!!
Why?!
I have to study for the exams.
I THINK... I'VE DONE SOMETHING STUPID DESPITE MYSELF.
IT'S TOO LATE TO TURN HIM DOWN...
But I do feel sorry about his dead girlfriend.
Hmmm.
WHAT SHOULD I DO?

GOOD EVENING. I'M HERE TO TAKE YOU TO THE PARTY, SIGNORINA.
I COULD NOT DO ANYTHING, AND THE DAY OF THE PARTY ARRIVED.
WE SHOULD ARRIVE EARLY SO I CAN HAVE YOU DRESSED UP.
Oh my.
He has a driver.
WHAT... IN THE WORLD ...?
Ah, chivalrous knights.
DON'T WORRY. I'VE ARRANGED A CAR FOR ALL OF YOU.
NOD.
LISTEN UP, PERVERT! WE'RE NOT LETTING SAKURA GO ALL BY HERSELF!

I'M GETTING REALLY NERVOUS...
ガラガラガラ
Ha ha ha.
THE MORE STAFF WE HAVE, THE BETTER.
?
Let us ride with Sakura.
Staff?
SIGNORINA, WAS TODAY'S SNACK DUMPLINGS?
HUH?
A COFFEE LOVER'S NOSE IS SPECIAL...
I'm sensitive to smell.
ちょん
あせあせ
Do I have stuff on my face?!
H-HOW DID YOU...?
Tee hee.
She loves dumplings.
...AND DUMPLINGS ARE MY FAVORITE.

This is "a small party"?
WHY THE HELL DO WE HAVE TO BE THE WAITERS FOR HIS STUPID PARTY?!
I'm sorry that you're being taken advantage of.
...IT'S NOT EASY TO BE OVER-PROTECTIVE, IS IT?
HMPH, I DON'T KNOW WHAT TO SAY, BUT...
PROFESSIONAL SMILE
Grr.
He's a pro.
くるり
OF COURSE, MA'AM.
EXCUSE ME, CAN I HAVE A DRINK?
ARE YOU TRYING TO PISS ME OFF?!
Huh?!
What'd I say?

WHISPER
HEY, HEY, HEY!
I JUST SAW A BIG GROUP OF TV STARS OVER THERE!
YES, BUT THERE SEEMS TO BE CELEBRITIES HERE, TOO.
This is that perv's party, right?
HMM?
.....
Celebrity
Celebrity
Celebrity
PRESIDENT?
Get back to work.
HE'S THE PRESIDENT OF A CAFÉ CHAIN. HE OWNS MORE THAN 100 CAFÉS ACROSS THE GLOBE.
Oh.
NATURALLY, HE HAS A LOT OF CONNECTIONS.
His charisma helps, too.
The TV stars and celebrities are all his friends.
Ume-chan.
IT REALLY IS LIKE MY FAIR LADY, ISN'T IT?
Is Sakura safe with him?!
SERIOUSLY, WHO IS THAT DUDE?!
My head hurts.
I DON'T KNOW, A RICH PLAYBOY?
I guess.

CLICK
I'm coming in.
SAKURA-CHA--
MAYBE WE SHOULD ALL HAVE GONE TO SEE...
...HOW SAKURA-SAN IS DOING, NOT JUST MASASHI.
They stayed to do their job.
THIS IS THE DRESSING ROOM, RIGHT?
SPEAKING OF A BRIDE...
JEEZ, I FEEL LIKE A BRIDE'S FATHER ABOUT TO SEE HIS DAUGHTER IN HER WEDDING DRESS.
...IN HER WEDDING DRESS...
...FUMIKO-SAN WAS SO BEAUTIFUL...

MASASHI?
GASP
OH, SORRY... I...

YOU'RE SO BEAUTIFUL ...
I KNOW THAT WHEN...
.....
BLUSH
That flower looks good on you.
YOU TOOK MY BREATH AWAY.
...MASASHI LOOKS LIKE THAT...
...HE IS...
...REMEMBERING THE DAYS WHEN MOM WAS ALIVE.
HUH, I USUALLY LOOK LIKE A CHILD TO YOU.
Ha ha!
BECAUSE YOU'RE CUTE AND WONDERFUL, TOO.

Thank you for picking up this book!! This book starts with the story of a man about whom my editor said, "seems like a pervert." I like men with beards, but this description must be due to my lack of drawing skill. There are some other reasons he's called a pervert, but let's have a big heart and forgive him, okay?

ME & A WEIRD MAN

I DON'T KNOW WHY, BUT BEFORE...
SHE LOOKS MORE AND MORE LIKE FUMIKO-SAN.
"YOU REALLY DO LOOK JUST LIKE HER."
...I DIDN'T REALIZE IT AT ALL.
NO... IT CAN'T BE.
I'm thinking too much.
.....

WHAT?!
I NEED YOUR ASSISTANCE FOR MY SPEECH.
Now...
table STOMP
A CAFÉ IS A PLACE WHERE PEOPLE CAN MEET!
SIGNORS, SIGNORAS, SIGNORINAS!!
I AM HONORED TO KNOW YOU ALL! YOU JOINED ME IN MY VARIOUS CAFÉS AND WE HAVE BECOME GREAT FRIENDS!
WE'LL KILL YOU LATER.
NOD
If he does anything more, we have no choice.
HA HA HA!
Jeez. Puku chan's strike zone is too wide.
JUST A FEW DAYS AGO, FOR INSTANCE, I FOUND THIS CUTE GIRL IN MY CAFÉ...

TREMBLE TREMBLE
Good for him.
She was cute.
Salute!!
TO OUR ENCOUNTER!
SALUTE!!
YOU MEAN IT'S ALL A LIE?!
HE MADE YOU GUYS WORK FOR HIM FOR FREE WITH HIS FISHY "LOVERS" TALE, DIDN'T HE?
WELL, HE'S COME THIS FAR WITH JUST HIS PERSONALITY.
It's also your dream to have your own shop, right?
WELL SAID, BUT IT ANNOYED ME ALL THE SAME. PERVERT.
"A café is a place where people can meet"?
You shouldn't step on a table with your shoes on.
Nice speech, wasn't it?
← Goodie two-shoes
BUT IT IS TRUE THAT THERE WAS A WOMAN WHO PASSED AWAY THAT HE CAN'T FORGET.
That's just what I think.
I DON'T KNOW.

?
GASP
Wa ha ha ha ha.
SORRY, I HAD TO GO TO THE BATHROOM.
You weren't working.
.....
WHAT TOOK YOU SO LONG, MASASHI?
WELL NOW, PRINCESS...
I'M WRAPPED AROUND HIS LITTLE FINGER.
No, it was me.
You told me you'd go out with me next, Taizo-san.
Ha ha... Let's go for a walk.
THIS IS STRANGE.
Sure.
Let's go to the Samba Carnival again.
Y-YOU...

MAY I HAVE THIS DANCE?
I don't know how to dance.
WHAT? BUT...
BUT...
NO BUTS.
LET'S DANCE.

...FOR SOME REASON...
...I DON'T HATE THIS MAN.
EVACUEES
They are Taizo's friends.
Sorry, guys!
Are you really a man? Let's strip him and see.
Eee! Help, Sakura-chan!
You wanna dance with me?
MAYBE BECAUSE ...
Play wit' me, hon.
...HE'S A BIT LIKE MASASHI.
Go away!
Two brothers who are harassed by drunks.

Don't tell me she is your really girlfriend!
S-SAYURI!!
?!
I'VE HAD ENOUGH!!!
I TOLD YOU TO THINK ABOUT MARRYING ME! WHY ARE YOU DANCING WITH SOME KID LIKE THAT?!
I CAN'T STAND IT ANYMORE!!
I'M THE ONLY ONE TAIZO-SAMA LOVES!!
NO!! TAIZO IS MINE!!
HEY! I'M TAI'S NUMERO UNO!!
WHAT ARE YOU TALKING ABOUT?! I'M THE ONE WHO'S MARRYING TAIZO!
WHAT?!
She's in junior high.
I'M SORRY, MY ANGELS.
BUT I'M CRAZY ABOUT THIS YOUNG GIRL.
SOME OTHER LUCKY, LUCKY GUYS WILL SOMEDAY MAKE YOU LADIES VERY HAPPY.
32
22
25
28

GRAB
WH-WH-WHAT A JERK!!
DIZZY
Could it be?
HE MADE ME PRETEND TO BE HIS LOVER JUST TO SAY THIS?
Shhh....
Its dangerous here!
IT LOOKS LIKE YOUR JOB IS OVER. LET'S ESCAPE.
Escape?
!
That jerk. I'll kill him someday.
ビタ
YOU JERK !!
HE DESERVES IT.
Please take your turn.
Ha ha ha. Good for you, Fukasawa-kun.

Me & My Brothers

Episode 16

I don't like drawing flowers. It's difficult.

HELLO!
GOOD TO SEE YOU AGAIN, SIGNORINA.
キキー
"That man"
!
TAIZO-SAN...
Speak of the devil.
WHAT?! WHO?! WHAT'S YOUR RELATION-SHIP?!
バタン

WHAT ARE YOU TALKING ABOUT?!
He's such a player!
You're cheerful and wonderful, too, signorina.
RELATIONSHIP? WELL, ALL I CAN SAY IS THAT WE'RE DESTINED FOR EACH OTHER.
You used me to ditch other women!
Wow.
HUH?!
OH, THAT'S RIGHT. I CAME TO APOLOGIZE FOR CAUSING YOU SO MUCH TROUBLE.
ポカーン
"OKAY"? GOOD, LET'S GO THEN.
Let me down!
Hee hee.
IT'S OKAY! YOU GAVE ME THAT DRESS! THAT WAS ENOUGH!!
NO, I DIDN'T MEAN...!

VROOM
ブロロロロロ
.....
Faculty
バタバタバタ
MIYA-SHITA-SENSEI!
びっくり
WHAT'S HAPPENED?
TANAKA-SAN, SUZUKI-KUN...
..AND MORISHIMA-KUN?

STOP!
PLEASE CALM DOWN, YOU THREE. I'M LISTENING.
TELL ME WHAT YOU SAW FROM BEGINNING TO END.
THAT GUY WAS REALLY WEIRD! HE WAS DRIVING A RED FERRARI! SERIOUSLY, HE'S A CREEP!!
SAKURA WAS HOISTED UP LIKE A PRINCESS BY A HANDSOME MAN! I'M SUPER-JEALOUS!
A GIGOLO TOLD MIYASHITA THAT THEY WERE DESTINED FOR EACH OTHER! SHE'S DEFINITELY BEEN TRICKED AND WE MUST RESCUE HER!!!
ぎゃあ
ぎゃあ
1
...TAKEN BY A SUPER-COOL GIGOLO MAN...
2
3
MIYASHITA WAS...
...IN SHORT, SHE WAS KIDNAPPED.
Buon giorno!
IT'S HIM...
...I THINK...
...I KNOW WHO THE KIDNAPPER IS.

カチャッ
What's up?
THIS IS AN EMERGENCY!!
ばっ
A red Ferrari, location unknown.
EVERYONE, SAKURA-SAN'S BEEN KIDNAPPED! WE HAVE TO RESCUE HER RIGHT AWAY!
ダッ
Got it!!
LaLaPizza
Senpai, you have a call from your brother.

THANK YOU ALL SO MUCH.
Sakura-san is blessed to have good friends.
What? "We"?
Yeeeah!
SENSEI, WE'LL LOOK FOR MIYASHITA, TOO!!
THIS IS FUN!
UH...
WHERE ARE WE GOING?
I'LL TAKE YOU TO THE END OF THE WORLD IF THAT'S WHERE YOU WANT TO GO.
ANYWHERE!

Whaat?! That's not fun, signorina.
AND ...
Go home.
THEN I WANT TO GO HOME.
I HAVE HOMEWORK TO DO.
Go home.
Go home.
He might really do that. Scary.
WHAT'S WITH HIM?
Tonight we're making dinner together.
...MASASHI IS WAITING FOR ME TO COME HOME.
Please watch the road!
WHA-WHAT ARE YOU TALKING ABOUT?!
Tee hee.
I SEE.
THAT KID IS THE CENTER OF YOUR UNIVERSE, EH?

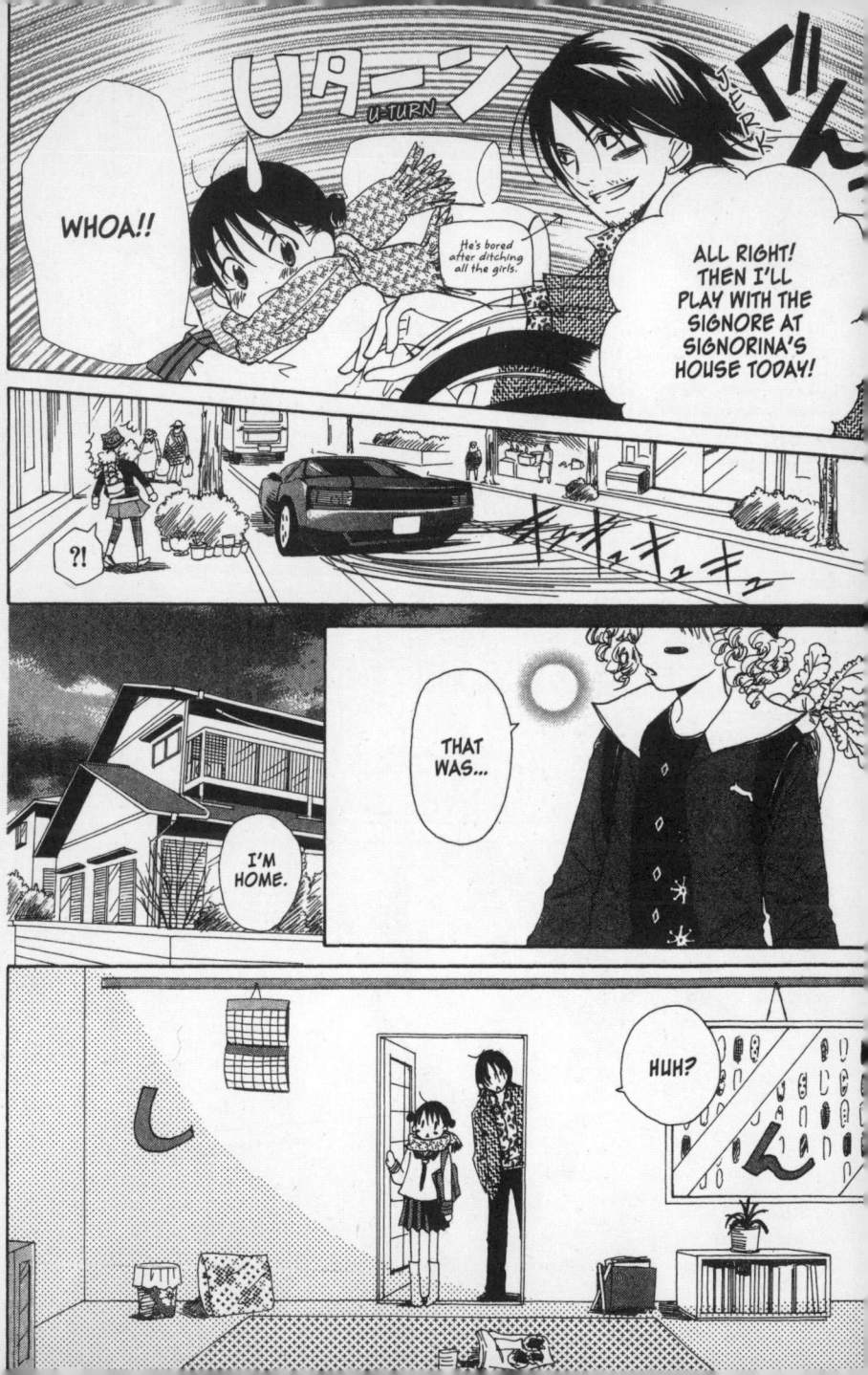
ユターン
U-TURN
WHOA!!
He's bored after ditching all the girls.
ALL RIGHT! THEN I'LL PLAY WITH THE SIGNORE AT SIGNORINA'S HOUSE TODAY!
?!
THAT WAS...
I'M HOME.
HUH?

おろ
ガラ
LOOKS LIKE HE'S OUT.
THAT'S WEIRD.
He's not here.

SEE? HE'S EXACTLY LIKE MASASHI.
HE MUST HAVE HAD AN UNEXPECTED ERRAND. THAT'S ALL.
Nooo!!
Here, jump into my arms in your despair!
No thanks.
HE BROKE A PROMISE?! SIGNORINA, OH, YOU POOR THING!!

SAKURA-CHAAAAAN! WHERE ARE YOU?!
Taizo Fukasawa, you idiot!
BUT HE USUALLY LEAVES A NOTE.
I WONDER WHAT HAPPENED.
I'm worried.
Are you lost?

PANT
Damn...
I HAVE TO THINK ABOUT WHERE TO LOOK.
IF HE TOOK HER IN HIS CAR, JUST LOOKING FOR HER LIKE THIS ISN'T GONNA WORK.
INNOCENCE LOST
TAKES HER TO HIS HOUSE
PLAYBOY
Jumping to a conclusion now.
イラ
イラ
イラ
イラ
イラ
イラ
イラ
イラ
THAT JERK... WHERE DID HE TAKE SAKURA?
HASN'T ANYONE SEEN THEM, AT LEAST?
SAKURAAAAAAAA!
Thus, Masashi became the wind.
Aaah!

TSUYOSHI!
キラキラ
.....
RIN?
WHAT ARE YOU...
...doing here?
I came here ta take the college entrance exam.
YA TOL' ME...
...TO COME A'GIN. REMEMBUH, TSUYOSHI?

TWITCH
I GUESS YA AIN'T INTERESTED THAT I SAW SAKURA-CHAN LOOK-ALIKE JUST NOW, EH?
What an attitude.
.....
OH, IT'S GREEN LIGHT NOW.
Gotta go.
<3
TSUYOSHI! ♡
So, where did you see Sakura? Tell me! Now!
I MISSED YOU, RIN!
Devious
TSUYOSHI'S GOT A LEAD!!!
Unexpectedly
I guess I have to, but there's no room for you.
IN TOWN, BUT I DUNNO WHAT STREET IT WAS. TAKE ME WITH YA, WILL YA? ♥

☆ 2 ☆

Well, ahem, I'm in trouble. I can't think of anything to write. So I'll introduce my sister again, I think. I have two sisters. When I made one of my sisters a clock in volume 3, the eldest sister said that if she had to be a clock, she wanted it to be antique.

I don't think she'll like it. She might get mad. But I couldn't think of another antique shape... But anyway, the space is filled and that makes everything okay.

Morishima residence
A RED CAR?
OH, YES, I THINK I SAW IT.
ANYWAY, PLEASE TAKE CARE OF SUGURU, MIYASHITA-SENSEI.
PLEASE COME IN AND HAVE DINNER WITH US, PLEASE.
Don't force him inside the house!
STOP IT, GRANDPA! YOU'RE EMBARRASSING ME!!
Uh, sir, this is not the time for...
Sensei!!
Pbbt!
I'M HOME...
...GRANDMA, DAD, MOM.
SIGNORINA'S PARENTS ARE GONE?
OH, SORRY. I'LL MAKE YOU TEA NOW.
I forgot.
THEN I'LL SAY HI TO YOUR PARENTS.
OH! THANK YOU!

Hm?
Wha...?
GASP
TAIZO-SAN, WHICH WOULD YOU LIKE? GREEN TEA, HOJI TEA OR GENMAI TEA?

STARE
OH, I JUST REMEMBERED AN ERRAND.
I HAVE TO GO NOW, BAMBINA.
Oh what a shame.
WHAT?
No tea?
?
はぁ
DID HE WANT COFFEE?
Arrivederci
?
?

NO WONDER SHE LOOKS SO MUCH LIKE HER.
SCRATCH SCRATCH
CLICK
.....
.....
CLICK
.....
トコ トコ
...SOMEONE WILL COME HOME SOON.
Rin-chan said she'd visit, but I wonder when?
NOW I'M ALONE.
I HOPE...

YOU DID THIS ON PURPOSE, DIDN'T YOU?
YOU SAID "IN TOWN"!! WHY THE HELL DID WE END UP BY THE OCEAN?!!
Waaaa!
I AIN'T GOT ANY IDEA, EITHER!
I didn't mean to!
Damn!
I'M SO ANGRY AT MYSELF FOR FORGETTING YOU HAVE A TERRIBLE SENSE OF DIRECTION!
IT'S OKAY... CONCENTRATE ON THE STREET WHERE YOU SAW SAKURA.
Calm down, calm down, Tsuyoshi.
I'LL GO LOOK FOR HER BY MYSELF.
Er...
I THINK...
Er...
...THERE WAS A SUPERMARKET NEXT TO A BAKERY, AND...

Oh!!
IT SAID, NIKO-CHAN MARKET MIDORIMACHI STORE!
WHAT?!! THAT'S RIGHT BY MY HOUSE!!!
DING DONG
DING DONG
Stupid auto lock!!!
ピピピ

HUG!!
HELLO, MR. MASASHI!!
I'M SO GLAD TO MEET YA!
I'm a big fan of yours!!
?!
Masashi is a novelist.
MIYASHITA?! MASASHI?!
Really ?!
COME IN!! PLEASE!!
BY THE WAY, MISTER, WHO ARE YOU?
Thanks
D-did I come to the wrong room?
Cleft chin No. 2
HUH.
That's nice of him.
TAIZO SUPPORTS PEOPLE WHO CHASE THEIR DREAMS.
SO TAIZO KINDLY LET ME LIVE IN HIS APARTMENT.
I CAME TO JAPAN TO STUDY, BUT I'M REALLY POOR, Y'KNOW?
My friend and I collapsed in Taizo's café.
CALL ME JACK.

Sash: TV Champ Best Tournament

!
THU-THUMP
THAT'S A PICTURE OF HIM WHEN HE WAS YOUNG.
I heard that he was on "TV Champ."
DO YOU LIKE THE PICTURE?
NO.
SORRY TO HAVE DISTURBED YOU. LOOKS LIKE SAKURA ISN'T HERE, SO I'M GOING HOME.
OH, WAIT!
BEFORE YOU GO HOME, I'LL TELL YOU ONE THING THAT I JUST REMEMBERED.

I HEARD THAT TAIZO ALWAYS TAKES GIRLS TO WHERE THEY WANT TO GO MOST.
YOUR SISTER MUST BE...
...SOMEPLACE SHE REALLY LOVES.
THANKS.
THEN THAT'S WHERE I'LL GO.

TIC TOCK TIC TOCK
EVERY-ONE IS...
...SO LATE TODAY.
Gya ha ha!
AT A TIME LIKE THIS...
...AND WHEN I WAS LEFT ALL ALONE, I FELT THE SAME WAY AS I DO NOW.
WHEN GRANDMA DIED...

むく
PEOPLE OFTEN FEEL SORRY FOR ME FOR NOT HAVING PARENTS.
AND THERE WERE TIMES I FELT LONELY.
...I REALIZE HOW FORTUNATE I'VE BEEN.
BUT I HAD GRANDMA, WHO WAS ALWAYS WITH ME...
...AND NOW I HAVE BROTHERS.
THAT'S WHY...
...I'M NOT REALLY USED TO BEING ALONE.
FLOP
JUST BECAUSE THEY'RE LATE... I'M SUCH A CHILD.

SO PLEASE ...
CLICK
...COME HOME SOON, EVERYONE.
ガ
ばっ
はあっ
I'M HOME!

SAKU--
ターン
Phew.
WELCOME HOME.

WHEN EVERYONE IS HERE, THIS HOUSE BECOMES MY FAVORITE PLACE.
I'm sorry! I missed you!
Long time no see.
I was gonna say that.
Phew.
YOU'RE ALL LATE.
I WAS WORRIED.
THE NEXT DAY ...
Was that what everyone thought yesterday?
Me, too. Sorry for making such a fuss.
Grandpa embarrassed me.
I-I'm sorry, guys.
WHAT? KIDNAPPED?!
I CAN'T BELIEVE YOU WERE HOME THE WHOLE TIME.
Yeah.
But I enjoyed it.

Me & My Brothers
Episode 17

...not too bad.
Hmm? This is...
Soy milk

CLANK
CLANK
IT'S NOT ME...
...you're making too much noise.
Takeshi-kun...
ARE YOU ALL RIGHT, TAKESHI?!
EARTH

OOOUCH.
MA-MASASHI?
ぺちょ

It isn't that unusual.
Yeah.
COMPARED TO SAKURA AND TAKESHI.
BUT IT'S UNUSUAL FOR YOU TO MAKE A MISTAKE LIKE THIS, MASASHI.
Pretending to be girly.
I WAS ORGANIZING THE CABINET AND LOST MY BALANCE.
EARTH
Heh heh.
DON'T TEASE TSUYOSHI-KUN TOO MUCH.
Sakura-san.
TAKASHI...
Why are you laughing?!
I'LL GO WASH TSUYOSHI'S UNDIES, I THINK.
I told you, I'll do it myself!
SORRY!! I'M SORRY!!!
Ah ha ha ha!
OH, THANKS! WE'RE DONE TALKING ABOUT THIS, OKAY?!
Please!
O-OKAY.
BY THE WAY, MASASHI...
...I FOUND THIS PICTURE ON THE KITCHEN FLOOR. WHO IS THIS?
!

SUSPICIOUS
?
WHOSE PICTURE IS IT?
.....
I CAN'T TELL YOU.
Sorry, Sakura-chan.
?!
Hmmm...
.....
I'm sure he's just thinking about something stupid again.
MASASHI IS ACTING STRANGE.
More than usual.
EARTH
NOW I HAVE TO GO TO MY ROOM AND WORK!

*The word "koi" (as in Koi fish) also means "love" in Japanese.

PACE
PACE
SIGH...
Masashi's room
SPLASH
THU-THUMP THU-THUMP THU-THUMP THU-THUMP
MAYBE I CAN SEE THE PICTURE WHILE MASASHI IS IN THE TUB...
NOW'S MY CHANCE!
BATHROOM
SPLOSH
SPLISH
.....
WHAT'RE YOU DOING, SAKURA?
YO, ARE YOU LISTENING?
Don't ignore me.
...FOR SOME REASON, I CAN'T SEEM TO FORGET IT.
Perhaps... he's in love.
IT'S NOT THAT I BELIEVE WHAT RIN-CHAN SAID, BUT...
SNEAK

トン
トン
トン
MASASHI ...
ARE YOU OUT OF THE BATH?
Panic
!
SLIDE
BATHROOM
?
Uh, um, uh, eh....
TS-TSUYOSHI...
BLUSH
DID SOMEONE JUST CALL ME?
カチャ
I'left a change of clothes in my room.
SURE, BUT WAIT UNTIL I PUT SOMETHING ON.
Oh, it's you.
I NEED TO TALK TO YOU. CAN I HAVE A MOMENT?

SLAM
HALL CLOSET
Tsuyoshi-kun left the TV on again.
HEY, WHAT'S GOING ON?
OH NO NO, IT'S NOT RIN-CHAN'S FAULT!
I'LL KILL HIM LATER.
I SEE... IT'S BECAUSE OF WHAT RIN SAID, ISN'T IT?
I'M SORRY... I WAS TRYING TO SNEAK INTO MASASHI'S ROOM BECAUSE I WANTED TO SEE THE PICTURE.
I hid because I felt guilty.
Honest girl

YOU WERE ALWAYS FOLLOWING MASASHI AROUND AND YOU'D CRY WHEN HE WASN'T THERE.
The center of Sakura's world was always Masashi.
JEEZ. YOU HAVEN'T CHANGED AT ALL SINCE YOU WERE A KID.
VACUUM
Hmph
YOU ALWAYS FAVORED MASASHI.
KINDA PISSES ME OFF.

MORON! THAT HAS NOTHING TO DO WITH OUR RELATIONSHIP!
YOU'RE THE ONE WHO DOESN'T LET ME WASH YOUR UNDERWEAR.
TH-THAT'S NOT TRUE!
I WONDER ...
...WHEN WE BECAME SO CLOSE?
A young girl like you shouldn't wash men's underpants.
He's old-fashioned.
...BUT NOW, I CAN CONFIDENTLY TELL EVERYONE IN THE WORLD...
...THAT MY BROTHERS ARE MY FAMILY.
THERE WAS A TIME WHEN I WORRIED ABOUT NOT BEING RELATED BY BLOOD...
SO? WHAT DID YOU WANT TO TALK ABOUT, TAKASHI?
SLAM
!

Idiot.
What?
Masashi...
BEFORE THAT, YOUR SHIRT IS INSIDE-OUT AND BACKWARD.
OH?!
ARE YOU STILL THINKING ABOUT THE PICTURE?
WHAT?
THAT PICTURE OF TAIZO FUKASAWA?

WHAAAT?!
Signorina.
I love you for you! Come here, signorina.
Ha.
I love you.
Tee hee.
No, no, that can't be!!!
I hope.
WHAT ARE YOU...
WE WERE WORRIED ABOUT A LOT OF THINGS HE DID, BUT...
...I DON'T THINK HE'S A BAD PERSON.
RUSTLE
.....
GLANCE
?
...THINKING, MASASHI?
IT'D BE A PROBLEM IF HE WAS A BAD PERSON.
YEAH.

I FOUND THIS WHEN I FORCED MYSELF INTO TAIZO FUKASAWA'S HOUSE.
I WAS SURPRISED AND TOOK IT WITH ME...
Go, Taizo!!
...BECAUSE FUMIKO-SAN WAS IN THE PICTURE WITH HIM.

"YOU LOOK EXACTLY LIKE MY GIRLFRIEND, WHO PASSED AWAY..."
THERE'S A CHANCE...
...THAT IT ISN'T SOME ACCIDENTAL RESEMBLANCE, RIGHT?
EARTH
ダン

SAKURA...
IS TAIZO-SAN MY...?
IT CAN'T BE.
WHAT ...
...DOES THAT MEAN?!

TO ME...
Hey.
IT CAN'T BE TRUE.
MY...
WOBBLE
EARTH
...IT WAS ALWAYS NATURAL NOT TO HAVE A FATHER.
Her knees gave way.
BUT I TOOK TOO LONG, I GUESS.
I WAS GOING TO MAKE SURE BEFORE I TOLD YOU.
I'M SORRY.
.....

I FELT...
...THAT ONCE YOUR REAL FATHER WAS FOUND, WE MIGHT BECOME USELESS.
THAT'S WHY I COULDN'T BRING MYSELF TO INVESTIGATE SOONER.
WHAT?! THAT'S JUST SILLY!
You looked up. Finally.
YEAH.
I KNOW. I'M SORRY.
THERE IS ONE MORE REASON WHY I WAS HIDING IT FROM SAKURA.
GRIN
I'LL NEVER LEAVE YOUR SIDE... NO MATTER WHAT HAPPENS.

トン
BLUSH
BUT...
...I DON'T WANT HER TO REALIZE THE POSSIBILITY.
MASASHI.
SNIFFLE
!
You were listening?
WHAT? IF YOU HAVE SOMETHING YOU WANT TO SAY, JUST SAY IT, TAKESHI.
.....
TAKESHI-KUN?
YESTER-DAY...
...UME-CHAN TOLD ME...

☆ 3 ☆

Er...uh...um... oh no, I don't know what to write! I guess I'll write about this manga. Let's see, let's see... Sakura-chan became a high school student in Episode 19. Surprising. It can't be helped because everyone looks young in my drawings, but...

...she's a little like an elementary student, isn't she? I'll try and make her grow up inside and outside. Also, I have to do something about all those new characters I created despite my lack of drawing skills. There are characters that only appeared in one episode.

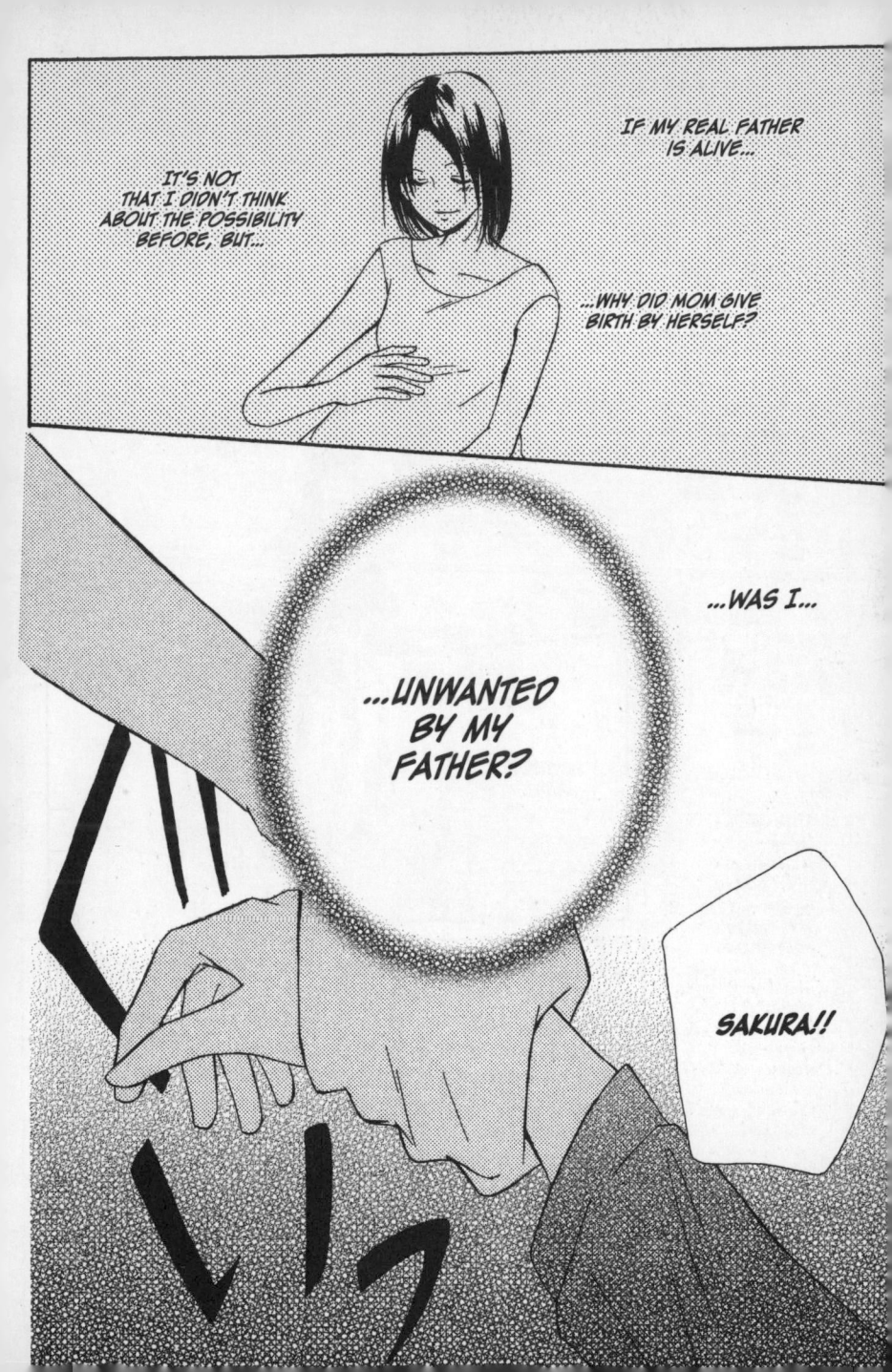
IT'S NOT THAT I DIDN'T THINK ABOUT THE POSSIBILITY BEFORE, BUT...
IF MY REAL FATHER IS ALIVE...
...WHY DID MOM GIVE BIRTH BY HERSELF?
...WAS I...
...UNWANTED BY MY FATHER?
SAKURA!!

THAT JERK... HE CAN'T GET AWAY FROM ME.
CRACK CRACK.
I'll kill him.
LET'S GO ASK HIM DIRECTLY...
...RATHER THAN IMAGINING UNNECESSARY THINGS.
COME WITH US, SAKURA-SAN.

I'LL BE ABLE TO ACCEPT ANY ANSWER.
YEAH.
I'LL BE ALL RIGHT AS LONG AS I'M WITH MY BROTHERS.
どさっ
ARE YOU REALLY LEAVING, TAIZO?
I'll miss you.
You can use this room as long as you want. Good luck. Jack.
...I DIDN'T KNOW THAT IT WAS GOING TO BE SO SOON.
I KNOW THAT YOU WERE PLANNING TO OPEN A CAFÉ IN ITALY, BUT...
Ha ha ha.
THE WORLD IS CALLING ME, JACK.
Big Apple

PLUS, IF I STAY IN JAPAN...
...I'LL BECOME TOO SENTIMENTAL.
AND THAT'S NOT LIKE ME...
...IS IT?

!
I'M HERE...
...TO ASK YOU A QUESTION.
SIGNORINA ...

I'M NOT RELATED TO MY BROTHERS BY BLOOD.
THE FATHER WHO WAS IN THE PICTURE ISN'T MY REAL FATHER.
ARE YOU MY MOTHER'S EX-BOYFRIEND, WHO LEFT HER 17 YEARS AGO?
YES, I AM.
!
AFTER ALL THAT...

...I'M NOT GOING TO CALL MYSELF YOUR FATHER.
BUT I'M AFRAID...
...I COULDN'T ESCAPE FROM A TRUTH THAT I DIDN'T WANT TO KNOW.
TSUYOSHI!!
...I CAN DO FOR HER AFTER ALL THESE YEARS.
WHY YOU --!!
THERE IS NOTHING...
I WON'T BE ABLE TO BE THE FATHER THAT YOU WANT ANYWAY.
ANYWAY...
...YOU WEREN'T IN MY LIFE BEFORE.
THAT'S FINE WITH ME.
CLENCH

...NEVER TALK ABOUT MY DAD?
WHY DOES GRANDMA...
SO, I'M ALL RIGHT.
THAT MAKES ME VERY HAPPY.
I GOT TO MEET SOMEONE WHO MAY BE MY REAL FATHER.
THAT IS ENOUGH.

VROOM
WELL?
BECAUSE...

I THINK THIS IS THE FIRST TIME IN MY LIFE...
...I'VE HAD REGRETS.
JEEZ...
WHAT HAVE YOU DONE TO ME, FUMIKO?
...I WAS ALWAYS HAPPY WITHOUT HIM.
LET'S GO HOME.

Me & My Brothers
Episode 18

"I'M NOT GOING TO CALL MYSELF YOUR FATHER."
TWO WEEKS HAVE PASSED SINCE TAIZO-SAN LEFT FOR ITALY, AND...
...TODAY IS MY JUNIOR HIGH SCHOOL'S GRADUATION CEREMONY.
Oooh!
Eep!

I hate bitter coffee.
I like mine sweet.
And I like middle aged men.
HARI.

VII
CONGRATULATIONS ON YOUR GRADUATION...
.....
I wanna die.
...SAKURA-CHAN. ♥

WHAAAT? I WAS VERY HAPPY WHEN YOU GUYS WORE COSTUMES FOR ME ON CHRISTMAS!
I thought that you'd like it, too.
AGH!
WHAT ARE YOU DOING, MAKING EVERYONE DRESS UP LIKE THIS?!!
IDIOT !!
Costumes?
...Miyashita-sensei?
BUT TAKASHI TEACHES HERE!
What if the other teachers see him?
Sensei...
Ohh...
Oh my!
You forced him to wear it, didn't you, Masashi?
OH.
Takashi is a teacher in this junior high.
I-I DON'T MEAN THAT YOU DON'T LOOK GOOD, I--
IDIOT.
IT DOESN'T LOOK GOOD ON ME, DOES IT?
I wanted to entertain you.
N-NO!
I forced Tsuyoshi, but, Takashi was happy to wear it!!
しゅん

Note: In Japan, at graduation, girls ask for the second button from boys they fancy.

AND THIS IS THEM ACTING LIKE THEY USUALLY DO... HMMM.
But you'll accept Takeshi's won't you?
I'm not wearing a boy's uniform so I don't have the second button to give you!
I don't want it.
Oh, no! I'm sorry! Sakura-chan.
I'll give you mine.
...THEY'RE ACTING THE SAME AS USUAL.
...I CAN KEEP SMILING BECAUSE ...
Don't cry, Okada-Sensei. We'll see you again.
I'm not sad. Humph.
Mr. Okada: homeroom teacher
SAKURA! COME HERE AND TAKE A PICTURE WITH OKA-SAN!
ドキッ
...AND I FEEL A LITTLE BIT SAD.
OH.
A PLANE...
SOMETIMES I REMEMBER TAIZO-SAN'S WORDS...

"I GOT TO MEET SOMEONE WHO MAY BE MY REAL FATHER. THAT MAKES ME HAPPY."
I KNOW...
Yep.
RIGHT?
Sakura-chan is definitely trying to act normal.
SOB
THIS IS TOO MUCH FOR SAKURA-CHAN, DON'T YOU THINK?
...THAT IT'S BEST TO ACCEPT, AND GIVE UP THINGS THAT I HAVE NO CONTROL OVER.
.....
You look good.
MAYBE WE SHOULD ALL GO TO ITALY.
Since it's spring break.
WHAT'RE YOU TALKING ABOUT?! ARE YOU CRAZY?!
WHAT?!

It's a serious scene but he's wearing a school uniform...

...TO DECIDE TO HAVE A BABY ALL BY HERSELF.
WHEN YOU THINK THAT WAY...
...SHOULDN'T YOU BE THE ONE WHO HATES FUKASAWA-SAN THE MOST?
OF COURSE I HATE HIM!!!
えっへん
I'd like to give him hell any way possible!!
Thank you so much for everything, sir.
BUT...
I DON'T CARE IF IT'S A SELFISH REASON.
...SAKURA-CHAN IS MY TOP PRIORITY NOW.

SAKURA WOULDN'T BE HERE IF IT WEREN'T FOR HIM, SO...
I GOT TO KNOW FUMIKO-SAN AND SAKURA...
...AND THAT'S WHAT COUNTS.
WAVE
...I'M MORE THANKFUL THAN ANYTHING ELSE.
GRR...
Caught Masashi's smile.

BUT STILL...
...IF THAT DOESN'T LEAD TO SAKURA'S HAPPINESS...
...IT DOESN'T MEAN ANYTHING.
CLICK
What's going on?
??
Kyaah!
Oooouch!
You're a man! Don't scatter flowers!
STOP MAKING SUCH A GRAND SPEECH IN THAT STUPID COSTUME!!
LET'S CALL JACK FIRST AND ASK HIM TAIZO'S ADDRESS IN ITALY.
RIIING
Pick up the phone already.
RIIING
RIIING
RIIING
RIIING
HELLO?
BEEP

WHEN...
...DID YOU COME BACK TO JAPAN?
WELL...
I ONLY KNEW ABOUT HER DEATH THROUGH SOMEONE ELSE, SO I'VE NEVER VISITED HER GRAVE BEFORE.
!
ABOUT TWO OR THREE DAYS AGO.

THAT'S MY STORY, ALL RIGHT?
.....
Ume is disgusted with me.
I CAN'T BELIEVE SHE'S REALLY MY CHILD.
BUT NOW THAT SHE'S CONFRONTED ME, I HAVE NO REASON TO RUN AWAY ANYMORE. THAT'S WHY I CAME BACK.
I WAS GOING TO RUN AWAY BECAUSE I THOUGHT SHE MIGHT REALIZE THE TRUTH...
THAT TIME...
...IF I HADN'T SEEN IN HIS FACE THAT HE WAS BLAMING HIMSELF...
"I'M NOT GOING TO CALL MYSELF YOUR FATHER."
BUT THAT'S NOT THE ONLY REASON YOU CAME BACK, RIGHT?
...I COULD HAVE PUNCHED HIM.

IF YOU CAME BACK JUST TO SEE SOMEONE WHO'S PASSED AWAY...
...YOU MIGHT AS WELL STAY HERE UNTIL YOU DIE.
YOU'RE CUTE, BUT HARSH.
Heh.
YEAH, THAT'S RIGHT.
EVEN IF FUMIKO FOUND ANOTHER MAN...
...I ALWAYS BELIEVED THAT I COULD SEE HER AGAIN.
IF I STAYED IN ITALY...

☆ 4 ☆

I've been doing things like the soccer club and studying soccer abroad and stuff, but I'm only a pseudo soccer fan who doesn't know much about it.

I love Shinji Ono. This is out of date, but I also love Miyamoto the Masked Man. (He was wearing a mask at the World Cup, wasn't he...?) I lived in Chiba for a long time, so I'm a JEF fan. I don't know what kind of team it is, but it makes me happy when they win.

THAT'S WHY...

...I MIGHT HAVE TO EXPERIENCE THE SAME PAIN. I DIDN'T WANT THAT.

...I NEED TO STAY CLOSE ENOUGH TO HER SO THAT I CAN GO SEE HER WHEN I WANT.

EVEN IF I DON'T HAVE THE RIGHT TO.

WORRY
SHOCK
MAD
Buon giorno
HI, SIGNORS! WHAT A COINCIDENCE!
びくっ
?!
COINCIDENCE?! WHAT'RE YOU TALKING ABOUT?! YOU'RE IN FRONT OF OUR HOUSE!
I'll kill you!
Oh, you're right. I just realized it, signor.
Seriously, I'll really kill you.
WHAT?

WHY IS TAIZO-SAN IN FRONT OF MY HOUSE?!
WHY?!
URP!!
WELL ...
GRRR...
I'M TELLING YOU...
...UNLESS SAKURA COMES OUT BY HERSELF, I WON'T LET YOU INSIDE OUR HOUSE!
!

IF YOU UNDER-STAND ...
...WAIT FOR A BIT.
BUT...
I AGREE.
IN THAT CASE, I'D CHALLENGE YOU TO... A DUEL.
I'll beat you.
BAMBOO SWORD
...IF YOU MAKE SAKURA CRY AGAIN...
...I'LL NEVER FORGIVE YOU--EVER.
YOU MEANT IT, DIDN'T YOU, TAKASHI?
OF COURSE.
He's Kendo level 4.
IT'S OKAY AS LONG AS YOU DON'T MAKE SAKURA CRY.
Didn't you mean it?
Well... I did, too, but...
You guys...
That's right, you bastard. I won't forgive you, either. I won't kill you, but a duel would be fine. A duel? Oh, that's right, Takashi is good at kendo. Anyway, I don't want to see Sakura cry. I hope that he came here to make her laugh.
!

...I CAME HERE JUST TO MAKE HER COFFEE.
キシ
DO WHATEVER YOU WANT.
BUT...
KNOCK KNOCK
SAKURA?
I-I'M NOT HERE!
I'M NOT.
I MEAN ...
BONK
...TELL HIM I'M NOT HERE.
BECAUSE I'M SCARED.

HEY...
I'M SCARED TO SEE HIM AND GET HURT AGAIN.
...SAKURA, DID YOU REALIZE...
...WE DIDN'T GO LOOKING FOR HIM?
ゴチ
HE CAME LOOKING FOR YOU.

"I WANT YOU TO SEE HOW WELL I'VE DONE, FOR HER."
HE'S NOT VERY HONEST, IS HE?
I WONDER HOW MUCH TRUTH THERE WAS...
...IN TAIZO-SAN'S GOOFY WORDS?
ガチャ
Don't worry, signor. I'll make you a sweet one.
What do you mean--you came here just to make coffee?!
That's not what I'm talking about!
H-HI...
PLEASE COME IN.
OKAY.

THANK YOU.
YOU'RE RIGHT. I'M CRAZY ABOUT COFFEE THOUGH.
Ha ha.
WHAT THE HELL?! ARE YOU CRAZY?!
By the way, yours is a cappuccino.
LET ME INTRODUCE YOU. THIS IS MY SOUL-MATE, COFFEE-CHAN.
"Coffee-chan"? What the hell?!
TRAY
Tee hee.
Oh.
Hi.
Grazie!
10-year-old Taizo
Buono.
Buono.
Taizo's papa
I THINK THAT HE SPENT MORE TIME IN THE CAFÉ THAN AT HOME.
HE'D TAKE ME TO AN ITALIAN CAFÉ ALL THE TIME.
MY DAD LOVED ITALY, EVEN THOUGH HE'D NEVER BEEN THERE.

WHEN MY FRIEND INVITED ME TO ITALY TO WORK IN A CAFÉ...
...I FLEW AT ONCE WITHOUT HESITATION.
Look, Fumiko! A rainbow!! The sky is blessing my path toward becoming a barista!
SO, MY DREAM WAS TO GO TO ITALY...
...AND OPEN A CAFÉ TO SERVE THE BEST COFFEE IN THE WORLD!
AFTER SO MANY YEARS I FINALLY REALIZED HOW SHE MUST HAVE FELT AT THAT TIME.
I HAVE NO RIGHT TO BE YOUR FATHER.
SHE SAW ME OFF WITH A SMILE.
...TAIZO-SAN LOOK THIS SAD.
I'VE NEVER SEEN...

THIS IS... GOOD.
.....
SIP

I COULDN'T MAKE FUMIKO GOOD COFFEE...
...BUT I'M GLAD...
...THAT I CAN FOR YOU.

Sorry to have bothered you.
ARRIVEDERCI...
...BAMBINA.
WAIT!!

I'VE MET MY BROTHERS...
PLEASE CALL ME...
I'M NOT "BAMBINA" OR "SIGNORINA."
...SAKURA-- THE NAME MY BROTHERS GAVE ME.
I can't see, dammit. Move.
...AND MY FATHER AGAIN.
I DON'T KNOW WHAT HAPPENED IN THE PAST.

IT'S NEVER TOO LATE.
AND IF I MAY...
...WHENEVER AND WHEREVER...
...I'D LIKE TO SEE YOU, DAD.

SAKURA, EH?
I'M SURE THAT MOM WANTED...
YEAH, FUMIKO LOVED THE SAKURA BLOSSOMS.
It's not blooming yet.
... REALLY WANTED ...
...DAD'S DREAM TO COME TRUE.
GOOD NAME.
YEAH.

SAKURA.
MOM, CAN YOU HEAR ME?

LOOK, SAKURA-CHAN.
THE CHERRY BULBS ARE GETTING BIG!
SPRING IS ALMOST HERE IN THIS WORLD.
THEY'RE SO TINY AND CUTE, AREN'T THEY?
It's a very good name.
IT'LL BE BEAUTIFUL THIS YEAR AGAIN.
Uh-huh.
What's wrong with you all?!
URRGH...
STOP LOOKING AT MY FACE AND TALKING ABOUT CHERRY TREES!
YEAH, IT'S ALMOST CHERRY BLOSSOM SEASON.

Me & My Brothers
Episode 19
An order for the love

So I think that it'd be better for you to be with your brothers. But come visit me anytime!
It's not morally good to live with me.

IZUMI HIGASHI HIGH SCHOOL.

THIS IS THE HIGH SCHOOL THAT TAKESHI ATTENDED UNTIL LAST YEAR.

I PASSED THE EXAM AND GOT ACCEPTED TO GO TO SCHOOL HERE.

I THINK I'LL GO GROCERY SHOPPING AFTER SCHOOL.

She's still like a housewife. She still looks like an elementary school kid.

Hey, let's go to gokon* someday, okay?

I-I'll pass.

Bye-bye.

But you don't know many boys.

Shut up!

* A gokon is a party where boys and girls meet.

If you'd like to send me comments about my book, here's the address:

TOKYOPOP
c/o Hyun Joo Kim
5900 Wilshire Blvd. Ste 2000
Los Angeles, CA 90036

Cool it with water.
WHOA! MY LEG IS SWOLLEN. SOMEBODY GET ME A COLD SPRAY.
OH, WE'RE OUT.
SUZUKI!
GO GET ME A GATORAID. QUICK!
I want Red Bull.
Anything!
GIMME A SECOND.
MY TOWEL IS GONE.
BY THE WAY, SUZUKI-KUN WANTED TO COME TO THIS SCHOOL BECAUSE THE SOCCER TEAM IS REALLY GOOD, AND...
...HE GOT IN AS WELL.
I'M SO THIRSTY THAT I'M GONNA DIE!
Naka-chan is also in the same high school, but she doesn't appear in this episode.
Me, too.
I SAW YOUR TOWEL IN THE CLUBROOM.
SUZUKI-KUN?
HM?
OH, WAIT, MIZUSAWA IS A FIRST-YEAR. GO WITH SUZUKI.
SHOOT, ALL THE OTHER FIRST-YEARS WENT RUNNING.
He can't possibly carry all the drinks by himself.
HELL NO! NO WAY!
CAPTAIN
THEN I'LL GO BUY DRINKS AND STUFF.

I'M THE RISING STAR OF THIS TEAM, YOU KNOW?!
I was scouted by the coach.
HE'S SO ANNOYING.
ACE STRIKER
WHY DON'T YOU MAKE THE SECOND-YEARS WHO AREN'T FIRST STRINGERS GO?
2nd year
Well, maybe I'll go then.
2nd year
I-I'LL BE FINE BY MYSELF...
I'LL HELP YOU WITH YOUR SHOPPING, IF YOU'D LIKE.
SUZUKI
SU--
SUZUKI-KUN.
WHOA! MIYA-SHITA!
MONEY BAG
LOOKS LIKE YOU'RE BUSY.

YOU WERE ASKED TO BE THE MANAGER?!
Manager
Star
Not that kind of manager.
SECOND BROTHER TAKASHI: TEACHER
ELDEST BROTHER MASASHI: ROMANCE NOVELIST
I-IT'S FOR MY FRIEND'S TEAM.
I see, the manager of a school club.
Oh, I'm sorry to hear that.
Green onion cut by Sakura.
THEY'RE HAVING A GAME SOON BUT THEIR MANAGER GOT INJURED.
FOURTH BROTHER TAKESHI: COLLEGE STUDENT
I WANTED TO HELP, AND ACCEPTED THE OFFER.
Hey! get the rice off your face already!
You're too nice.
THIRD BROTHER TSUYOSHI: FULL-TIME PART-TIMER

☆5☆

Two more of these 1/4 columns. Oh well, I've run out of things to write again. Then let's talk about my family. My parents are leading a country life. They even built their own house.

They raise fancy chickens and their eggs are delicious. Thank you for sending them to me! If you buy this type of chicken's eggs at the store, they cost...

...500 yen each! !!

Each! Not per carton!

Even though I'm not a gourmet, I think these eggs are delicious.

Does this column sound gossipy?

SOCCER CLUB.
UH... IT'S... S--

Ooh! She's really tiny!
SHE'S GOING TO LOOK AFTER US WITH THIS TINY BODY, SO BE THANKFUL.
THIS IS SAKURA MIYASHITA. SHE'LL BE OUR MANAGER UNTIL THE GAME.
I'm bored.
"NANA & NENE," THE TEAM'S IDOLS.
Just kidding.
AND HE'S HER TWIN BROTHER, NANA KOZUKA.
SHE'S THE INJURED MANAGER, NENE KOZUKA, A SECOND-YEAR.
Do you want me to sing?
Twins
WILL YOU PLEASE STOP TELLING STALE JOKES?
It's a waste of time.
Nice to meet you.
I'M TERADA, THE CAPTAIN. I'M A THIRD-YEAR.
Why you...
AND THAT FEEBLE LOOKING GUY IS OUR COACH.

I'LL EXPLAIN THE JOB. PLEASE COME WITH ME.
She's beautiful!
OH, RIGHT.
That wasn't nice.
Suzuki-kun
EXPLAIN THE JOB? SHE'S OUR ERRAND GIRL! THAT'S ALL, RIGHT?
Hurry.
Let's go.
What?
CLAP CLAP
HEY, KID, I'M HUNGRY. GO GET ME SOMETHING.
MIZU-SAWA !!!
I'M SORRY YOU GOT INVOLVED, MIYASHITA!
Here! Why don't you eat my left-over lunch?
"Errand girl" is fine.
DON'T WORRY, SUZUKI-KUN. I'M ALL RIGHT.
OUR NEW STRIKER IS TROUBLE.
SINCE HE'S SO GOOD, COACH DOESN'T SAY ANYTHING.

I-I'M NOT LIKE...
Be with who?
NOW, THIS IS YOUR FIRST JOB.
IF YOU ACCEPTED THE JOB JUST BECAUSE YOU WANTED TO BE WITH HIM...
HUH?
...OR YOU JUST WANTED TO BE SURROUNDED BY BOYS, YOU BETTER QUIT NOW.
?!
CLEAN THE CLUBHOUSE, PLEASE.
STINKY

THAT'S ALL YOU NEED TO DO FOR TODAY.
YOU DON'T KNOW HOW TO GIVE FIRST-AID OR HOW TO TAPE ANYONE UP, DO YOU?
ANYWAY, YOU DON'T NEED TO COME BACK TO THE FIELD UNTIL YOU FINISH.
SEE YOU LATER THEN.
It stinks...
もわ
バタン
Urp.
P-PLEASE DON'T CLOSE THE DOOR...
I have to get some fresh air or I'll die.
SLIP
?!
ずべっ
TRASH

GASP
RUSTLE
THIS...
SLAM
THIS IS...
KATHUNK
...EXCITING!!!
...RATHER...
I'm good at...
...cleaning.

ぬぎ
ぬぎ
HEY, THAT TINY KID'S PRETTY USEFUL.
OOH! IT'S CLEAN!!
ガチャ
ガチャ
YEAH, THIS ROOM IS ACTUALLY INHABITABLE NOW.
I'M GLAD THAT I WAS OF SOME HELP.
TIDY
スッキリ

I'LL GO CHANGE, TOO. EXCUSE ME.
BOW
Living with my brothers made me used to this.
HUH?
?
SQUEEZE

I wonder if everyone's home by now.
IT'S SO LATE. MASASHI MUST BE COOKING DINNER BY HIMSELF.
ギャアキャア
MIYA-SHITA...
SHE SAW MY UNDER-WEAR!
Do you wanna see mine, too?
I see your under-wear every day.
She's a Peeping Tom!
IT'S LATE. I'LL WALK YOU HOME.
Let's go home together.
MIYASHITA!
SUZUKI-KUN!
THAT'S QUITE ENOUGH, BOYS!
First-years are so cute.
WH-WHAT ARE YOU GUYS TALKING ABOUT?!
FORGET SUZUKI. WHY DON'T YOU GO OUT WITH ME?
My name is Sako.
Jerk.
DUDE, STOP FLIRTING.
WHISTLE

IF YOU'RE GOING TO BOTHER MY SAKURA...
This is fake.
...YOU'LL HAVE TO GO THROUGH ME FIRST!!!
A YAKUZA BOSS-LADY?!
Eee!

Tsuyoshi-kun...
YO, YO! STEP UP IF YA WANNA DIE!
Jeez...
I WANNA CRY.
WHAAAT?! IT'S YOU WHO SAID HIGH SCHOOL KIDS NOWADAYS WOULDN'T BE SCARED UNLESS WE WENT THIS FAR!
DAMMIT! EVEN SAKURA IS SCARED!! NOW WHAT ARE WE GONNA DO?!
?!
No, Sakura!! This is just a lighter!
CLICK
You sissy!

EXCUSE ME, BUT ARE YOU SHOOTING A TV SHOW OR SOMETHING?!
Kyah!
I DON'T MIND BEING KILLED BY YOU!
WHAT THE...?!
HEY, WHAT DO YOU MEAN?!
どすん
KYA!
KYA!
UMPH!
WHOA!
ARE YOU ALL RIGHT, SAKURA-CHAN?
くいっ
I can't believe they pushed you off.

カーッ
Oh.
I'M...
...FINE! LET ME GO!!
HEE!
I'M GLAD I WASN'T THAT POPULAR!
Oh, Gosh!
You're so cute!
BOSS-LADY...
TWINKLE
TWINKLE
Whaat?!
He was somewhat popular after all.
Your husky voice is so sexy!!
WHAT?
MIZU-SAWA ?!
I'M IN LOVE WITH YOU, BOSS-LADY!!!
IF IT'S YOU, I DON'T MIND BEING SCOLDED!!!
Husky voice? He's a man!!
IT'S FOR YOUR SISTER'S SAKE, TOO.
HE'S A FIRST-YEAR, BUT HE'S GOT A BIG HEAD.
EGO-MANIAC?
Give him a good scolding.
MA'AM, HE'S AN EGO-MANIAC. PLEASE TEACH HIM A LESSON.
Listen!

YAKUZA MANGA
YAKUZA
I LIKE LIVELY KIDS, BUT...
I HEAR YOUR HEAD'S GETTING ALL BIG THINKING YOU'RE SOME BIG-SHOT.
MIZUSAWA...
Ooh! Your legs are so beautiful!!
I'M SORRY, MA'AM!
Raaaa!!
...I HATE MEN WHO DON'T KNOW HONOR!!!
NO, I DON'T.
Neither does my brother.
DO YOU THINK MIZUSAWA KNOWS WHAT "HONOR" MEANS?
NO WAY, SIR!!
THEN GO BUY ME A DRINK. THAT IS AN ORDER.
.....
I'LL LIVE FOR HONOR FROM NOW ON!!
Good.
Whatever.

Wow...
PLEASE POLISH THESE BALLS TODAY.
Where did they go?
The others...
Tsk.
I'D KILL THEM IF THIS WAS REAL.
Calm down, Tsugumichi-kun!
SO PLEASE CALL ME ANY TIME.
IF THERE ARE THINGS THAT YOU CAN'T DO WITH ONE ARM, I'LL HELP.
There is not much I can do, but...
OH, WAIT!
YOU DON'T HAVE TO DO ANYTHING ELSE UNTIL YOU FINISH IT.
くるっ
スタスタ
スタスタ
WOW.
LITTLE BY LITTLE...
TO BE HONEST, I'M HAPPY THAT YOU'RE HERE. I KNOW IT'S HARD WORK, BUT LET'S DO OUR BEST TOGETHER.
Y-YES.
THANKS.

...I'M GETTING TO KNOW THE PEOPLE ON THE TEAM.
Samurai-hairdo.
HEY!
YOU'RE POLISHING THE BALLS FOR US?! THAT'S GREAT!
Stop playing with my hair.
GUYS, SAY THANK YOU TO HER NOW THAT YOU DON'T HAVE TO DO IT TODAY.
Wow! Lucky!
These two are probably good friends.
THIS IS FUN.
Captain!
Nene is so cool. I kinda wanna be like her.
OOOOH!
I'll do it!
Nice job, manager!!
Hooray!
I'm glad that's put up with errands and basic training!
IF YOU DO WELL, I'LL LET YOU PLAY IN A REAL GAME!
NOT ONLY THAT! NOW THAT YOU FIRST-YEARS HAVE EXTRA TIME, I'LL LET YOU JOIN THE GAME TODAY!!
RUB RUB
GOOD FOR YOU, SUZUKI-KUN.
EXCITED
YEAH, THIS IS A GREAT OPPORTUNITY!
THANKS TO YOU, MIYASHITA.
Heh heh. I'm so happy.
I'LL DO MY BEST.

IF I CAN BE...
AND...
...THIS IS REALLY NICE.
Go, Suzuki!
...USEFUL AND NEEDED BY SOMEONE...
LIBRARY BOOK
Ankle Taping
Point 7
I HAVE ONLY A FEW DAYS LEFT, BUT I WANT TO LEARN HOW TO TAPE SOMEONE UP.
Then I can be more useful.
I need the boss-lady!! Ask her to come to see the game, okay?!
Okay, okay.
...THAT'S A GREAT THING, ISN'T IT?

"How to Tape Someone Up"?
GASP
YOU'RE REALLY INTO IT.
OH, DEAR.
Hmmm.
How to Tape Someone Up
DON'T WORRY, I DON'T HAVE ANY BOOBS.
WHEN IT'S YOU, I'M EMBARRASSED FOR SOME REASON!
Hey!
I TOLD YOU TO PUT SOMETHING ON WHEN YOU GET OUT OF THE BATH!
SNORE
SNORE
But it's hot.
I'll put something on then.
SAKURA.

IF YOU'RE ENJOYING IT, YOU CAN CONTINUE YOUR MANAGER JOB, YOU KNOW.
I'LL DO THE HOUSEWORK.
YOU GO TO SCHOOL AND ENJOY YOUR SCHOOL LIFE, OKAY?
ENJOY SCHOOL LIFE?
IT IS TRUE...
Ankle Taping
...THAT I WAS HOPING TO CONTINUE.
SAKURA-SAN?

SOB
HUH?
IT'S WEIRD.
AND I KNOW MASASHI SAID THAT BECAUSE HE CARES ABOUT ME.
DON'T WORRY.
I WON'T TELL ANYONE.
D--
DON'T TELL MASASHI, OKAY?
THEN WHY...
...AM I FEELING SO LONELY?

DAY OF THE GAME
IZUMI HIGASHI'S ROOM IS OVER HERE.
YOU'RE QUITTING TODAY?! STOP KIDDING ME, DORK.
IF YOU QUIT, I CAN'T SEE BOSS-LADY ANYMORE.
Now, now, Mizusawa...
SO WHAT?
Not my problem.
WHAT DO YOU MEAN, "SO WHAT"?
Oh, my God. I'm in the second string.
I WON'T ACCEPT IT. IF YOU'RE QUITTING...
...I WON'T PLAY TODAY'S GAME.
WHAAAT?!
WHAT ARE YOU GONNA DO NOW? UTTER DEFEAT WITHOUT THE ACE, DON'CHA THINK?
IF YOU DON'T WANT TRAGEDY TO STRIKE, SHUT UP AND BE OUR ERRAND GIRL FOREVER!
Don't leave!

Here we are.
THAT'S...
...ENOUGH!
パシ
チーン
WHA...?!
?!
EVEN IF IT'S A JOKE...
...YOU SHOULD NEVER SAY THINGS THAT BELITTLE EVERYONE'S EFFORTS!!
Huh?
S--
SORRY.
Oh my
Sob!
She's like a mother!!
Don't worry. I did tell "her" to come here.
IF I STAY ON THE SOCCER TEAM AND WORK HARD WITH EVERYONE...
Good

...IT'LL BE FUN.
BUT MORE THAN THEM...
Go! Go!
IZUMI EAST
STOP IT ALREADY.
I TOLD YOU SO FROM THE BEGINNING.
PLUS, I REALIZED THE REASON...
...IT'S MY BROTHERS WHO I WANT TO BE USEFUL FOR.
Hey, he's good.
ARE YOU SURE YOU DON'T WANT TO CONTINUE THE MANAGER'S JOB?
Hm.
...WHY I FELT LONELY THAT TIME...

...AND WHY...
GIVE ME YOUR EAR, SAKURA-CHAN.
...I'M ALWAYS EMBARRASSED ONLY BY MASASHI.
TO BE HONEST, I WAS FEELING LONELY, SO I'M REALLY, REALLY HAPPY.
WHA...?!

Me & My Brothers 4 / End

How to Go Through a Secret Door

Me & My Brothers

はあっ
THIS IS A MYSTERIOUS STORY...
...WHERE A DREAMY GIRL FINDS THE DOOR OF TRUTH AND FICTION.
MONTHLY
LaLa
Chika Terashima: 10th grade
Idiot, idiot, idiot.
バカバカ
THAT'S WHY YOU DON'T HAVE A BOYFRIEND.
THERE ARE NO PRINCES.
Shohei Terashima: 10th grade
(Her fraternal twin. (He's the younger brother.)
I WANT TO LIVE SURROUNDED BY PRINCES LIKE HIM... ♥
Tono... Ryo-sama... Mika is cool, too... and... and...
Princes in LaLa.
ぅぉとり
Ew.
YOU'RE SUCH AN IDIOT.
WHAT?! IS YOUR FRIEND HERE?!
Stop calling me an idiot! I'm your big sister!
RIGHT?
ガーン

OH, IT'S ONLY TOMO-CHAN. YOU FREAKED ME OUT BECAUSE I'M IN MY PJS.
What's up?
They've been friends since elementary school.
OTHERWISE YOU'LL NEVER RETURN IT. YOU'VE BEEN THAT WAY SINCE YOU WERE A CHILD.
Don't point.
HE SAYS HE WON'T GIVE ME THE NEW JUMP UNTIL I RETURN HIS CD.
BUT YOU DON'T HAVE A GIRLFRIEND, EITHER.
Don't ask me.
Tomoya Okubo: 10th grade
STOP SAYING RUDE STUFF AND JUST RETURN THE CD, YOU JERK!
BUT I DIDN'T SAY BALLS!
Yow!
KEH. YOU'RE TOO FUSSY FOR A GUY.
DO YOU EVEN HAVE 'NADS?
Jeez.
JEEZ. YOU FANTASIZE ABOUT MEN TOO MUCH...
ANNOYED
...BECAUSE YOU GO TO AN ALL-GIRLS SCHOOL.

I'm not even gonna answer anymore.
Let's go to my room, Tomo.
HEPH.
YOU SHOULD COME TO OUR SCHOOL ONCE.
That'll wake you up for sure.
IDIOT! THEY REALLY ARE SWEET AND INNOCENT!
SHUT UP! YOU BELIEVE THE GIRLS ON TV ARE INNOCENT BECAUSE YOU GO TO AN ALL-BOYS SCHOOL!
SHOHEI... CO.
I'D GO LOOK FOR A PRINCE IF I COULD.
But we can't pull off a "switch." We don't look alike.
FWIP
She actually thought about it before.
"THE DOOR OF SOUL"...?
1. Believe in soul.
2. Believe in destiny.
3. Believe in the future.
4. Believe in the past.
5. Believe in fantasy.
The door will open to you if you believe in all, and lead you to the place you hope to go.
Door of Soul
But I bought it from a second-hand bookstore. Lucky me.
WHAT'S THIS? LALA'S SUPPLEMENT?
ひょい

The publisher has nothing to do with it...
Stop it, publisher!
WHOA! THIS IS CREEPY!!
Even I don't believe stuff like this!!
FADE
Oh, it's scary.
"2. BELIEVE IN DESTINY." DEFINITELY! I DO BELIEVE THAT!
Mmm.
"1. BELIEVE IN SOUL." YEAH, SURE. I'M SCARED OF GHOSTS.
NOW, WHERE DO YOU WANT TO GO?
BUT IF YOU'VE FOUND THIS PLACE, YOU MUST BELIEVE IN IT ALREADY.
HUH? WASN'T THERE ONE MORE BELIEF?
WHERE DO YOU WANT TO GO?
"3. BELIEVE IN THE FUTURE. 4. BELIEVE IN THE PAST."

...AND SNEAK INTO HIS SCHOOL, IT'D BE FUN.
CREAK
WELL, IF I COULD SWITCH WITH SHO-CHAN...
LET'S SEE.
ぱっ
I have to pee.
SHIVER
I HAD A WEIRD DREAM...
...AND WHY HAVE I FALLEN OFF THE BED LIKE SHO-CHAN?

Something's missing between my legs.
Huh?
びっ
Hmmm? What's this?
むく
WHAAAT ?! IT'S ME!!
GAAAH!
YAAH!
バターン
WHOA-!!
I'm acting like a girl! Eeew!

ドスドス
GET DRESSED AND GO TO SCHOOL ALREADY!!
SHE'S RIGHT.
WHAAT?!
ゴン ゴン
SHUT UP.
OH, COME ON. SHUT UP.
H-H-H-H-HEY, SHO-CHAN?! YOU'RE SHO-CHAN, RIGHT?
Why are you accepting it so easily?
It's my body though.
ピローン
...I CAN GO TO THE GIRLS' SCHOOL...
...AND YOU CAN GO TO THE BOYS' SCHOOL.
WHICH MEANS...!
I DON'T KNOW WHAT'S GOING ON, BUT I BECAME YOU AND YOU BECAME ME, RIGHT?

DREAM...? CAN IT BE THAT WHAT THE BOOK SAID WAS REAL?
BUT ...
THU-THUMP. THU-THUMP. THU-THUMP. THU-THUMP.
.....
THIS IS GREAT.
This must be a dream.
If so, I'll enjoy it!
Girls nowadays...
See ya lata!
THERE. GO ENJOY YOURSELF.
PAT
Tee hee.
.....
...IF SO, I'M SO LUCKY!
Stupid twins...

ギンッ
CHIKA-CHAN IS WALKING LIKE SHOHEI TODAY.
I WANT TO OBSERVE EVERYTHING ABOUT THE BOYS' SCHOOL. I CAN'T GIVE AWAY MY IDENTITY.
Y-YO, T-TOMOYA!
NICE DAY, ISN'T IT?
GASP
TOMO-CHA--
I mean...
WHAAT?! BUT IT'S LIKE EVERY GIRL'S DREAM TO SNEAK INTO A BOYS' SCHOOL, YOU KNOW?!
I'm grumpy.
His usual.
Eep!
I THINK THIS IS THE FIRST TIME SINCE ELEMENTARY SCHOOL I'VE SEEN YOU SO HAPPY IN THE MORNING.
GA HA HA HA HA!
.....
TH-THAT'S WHAT CHIKA SAID, AND I THOUGHT MAYBE OUR SCHOOL ISN'T SO BAD.
HALT

WELL...
...YOU'RE ALWAYS WEIRD ANYWAY.
GLANCE
NERVOUS
H-HE DIDN'T NOTICE, DID HE?
Well, it's impossible.

BOYS' SCHOOL, HERE I COME!!!
Phew.
Don't ask me.
THAT'S RIGHT! I'M WEIRD!!
RIGHT?!
OOH, FINALLY!!

Boys playing like puppies!!
OH, WOW... IT'S R-REALLY JUST GUYS.
The real feelings of boys in love!!
I pretend to be a playboy, but actually, I can't even hold the hand of the girl I like because I don't want her to hate me.
AND NOW I'M GOING TO ENTER THE CLASSROOM!!
Finally!!
And just lots of beautiful boys!!!

THERE WAS A DIFFERENT WORLD...BEHIND THE DOOR.
...how boys are in manga...
This is not...
Apologies to manga artists.
STIIIINK
WOBBLE
PULL
OH? YOU LOOK REALLY SICK, SHOHEI.
Morning.
HE'S WEIRDER THAN USUAL TODAY.
IT'S FILTHY!
AND SOMETHING SMELLS FUNNY.
UGH.
If you go to boys' school, I'm sorry.
WHAT THE HELL?
Makes no sense.
Oh, I feel a bit better.
WE'VE DECIDED THAT HE HAS THE SMELLIEST FEET IN THE CLASS.
OH, IT'S YOSHIDA'S FEET.
THUD
Bwa ha!
THIS ROOM SMELLS FUNNY.

I've run out of patience. If you don't pay me back, I'll follow you everywhere all day, even to the bathroom!
GIVE ME BACK THE MONEY YOU BORROWED FOR LUNCH ALREADY!
TERASHIMA, YOU BASTARD!!
?!
I... I'M SORRY...
I'll pay you back right away.
I don't want that...
SHO-CHAN, YOU IDIOT!
!!
Empty!!
Sho-chan's wallet
THU-THUMP
THU-THUMP
WHA-WHAT WAS THAT? TERASHIMA LOOKED AWFULLY CUTE JUST NOW.
"Thu-thump"? Did my heart say "thu-thump"?
HUH?
Keh Keh.
WHIMPER
Usually...
But now...

I-I'LL DO ANYTHING FOR YOU, SO...
Why do I have such a stupid brother?
I-I-I...
I'M REALLY SORRY!
She holds his hand so he can't punch her.
THEN WHY DON'T YOU MAKE SHOHEI DO YESTERDAY'S HOMEWORK FOR YOU?
You haven't done it yet, right?
Wake up, Hashimoto.
WHAT?
A-ANYTHING...? BUT YOU...
IF YOU NEED HELP, TELL ME, OKAY?
SHOHEI.
What's wrong with me?
TH-THAT WAS SCARY.
My knees gave way.

☆6☆

This is the last column. My parents liked this short story! (So embarrassing!) They liked it because it's a fantasy like Doraemon. (Seriously, it's embarrassing!!) People who don't usually read manga, like my parents, relatives and friends, buy my manga and read it. It's embarrassing to death but I'm happy to death at the same time. Of course, I most appreciate you fans who picked up this book. Hope to see you again.

Hari Tokeino

FLIP
XXX
For B and Over
Thanks.
SIR, I'LL TAKE HIM TO THE NURSE'S OFFICE.
GULP
CARE-TAKER
HMMM? WHAT'S THE MATTER, TERASHIMA?
CLANK
You're always hyperactive.
I don't know if it's unbelievable, but...
.....
...DO YOU READ THINGS LIKE THIS, TOO, TOMOYA?
This is unbelievable.
.....
SURE.
XXX
I brought it with me.
THE NURSE IS NOT HERE.
H-HEY...

Use scissors!

SHING
(What's this sound?)
NO?
Are you blushing, Tomo-chan?
HEY...
WILL YOU SEW MY BUTTON, TOO, TERASHIMA?
?!
A PRINCE!!
YES, OF COURSE!!
THERE HE IS!!
Do you wanna produce that sound, too? I'll give you a tip.
YEAH, A BEAUTIFUL BOY AND A NURSE'S OFFICE GO TOGETHER WELL, RIGHT?
ARE YOU DITCHING CLASS AGAIN, SASAHARA?
What's that weird sound?
At last!! The bed in nurse's office looks like a deluxe bed with a canopy!!
I KNEW IT! I KNEW IT! IT'S ONLY NATURAL THERE IS A PRINCE OR TWO AMONG ALL THESE BOYS!
Yes!!

NOW I'LL HAVE TERASHIMA SEW MY BUTTON. WHY DON'T YOU GO BACK TO CLASS?
Whoa.
YOU'RE NOT THE TYPE TO DITCH CLASS.
.....
ARE YOU ALL RIGHT ALONE, SHOHEI?
OH, YEAH. I-I'M SORRY THAT YOU HAD TO LEAVE THE CLASS FOR ME.
I'LL GO THEN. YOU GO BACK TO YOUR CLASS, TOO, ONCE SHOHEI GETS YOUR BUTTON BACK ON, OKAY?
OKAY, OKAY.
B-BUTTON... WHICH BUTTON IS MISSING?
THE PRINCE IS TOO CLOSE!
Uh uh uh uh...

WELL, AREN'T YOU QUITE THE FRIENDLY GUY TODAY, TERASHIMA?
You're usually colder.
THU-THUMP
STIFF
OH, NO...
I'M SHO-CHAN. I'M A MAN NOW... BUT MY FACE IS BURNING.
THU-THUMP
THU-THUMP
I see...
OH, BUT MAYBE HE'S THE PRINCE...
...I'VE BEEN LOOKING FOR.
GRIN
DREAMY
Dreamy girl

HOW'S TERA-SHIMA?
I TOOK HIM TO THE NURSE'S OFFICE. SASAHARA WAS THERE, TOO.
HE'LL BE FINE IF HE TAKES A GOOD REST.
WHAAT?!
In the nurse's office?!
SASAHARA?! DID YOU LEAVE HIM ALONE WITH MIZUKI?!
Mizuki Sasahara
SHAKE
SHAKE
HASHI-MOTO.
OKUBO.
STAND OUTSIDE.
WHY?
WHAT'S THE PROBLEM IF TWO MEN ARE LEFT ALONE?
I WOULDN'T BE WORRIED IF IT WAS THE USUAL TERASHIMA, BUT...
...TODAY'S TERASHIMA SHOULDN'T BE WITH MIZUKI.
TERASHIMA.
OH, NO. MY HEART CAN'T STAND IT.
I'd better finish the button business quickly.
?
THU-THUMP THU-THUMP THU-THUMP
UH, THE BUTTON...

Childhood friend
Real what?
MIZUKI IS A REAL...
Real...real...!!
?!
BEFORE YOU PUT THE BUTTON ON...
...I NEED TO UNBUTTON YOU.

UH, I-I'M A M-MAN (FOR NOW), YOU KNOW?!
Ah ha ha ha ha. What kind of joke is this?
SLIP
OF COURSE YOU ARE.
OTHERWISE I WOULDN'T BE INTERESTED.
HE'S GAY?!!
A twist!
Sho-chan's virginity is in danger!
I won't let you get away!
Some prince!
HUH?

I DON'T WANT THIS!
TOMO-CHA--!
OOPS.
Busted.
SASA-HARA.
PANT
GET YOUR HANDS OFF HIM RIGHT NOW OR I'LL BEAT YOU UP!
PANT

Ooh, scary.
!
RELEASE
Hashimoto-kun also came.
WHAT THE HELL ARE YOU DOING?!
Why is his shirt open?
OUCH... WHAT WAS THAT FOR?!
I haven't done anything yet, dammit.
TOMO-CHAN!!
I was scared!
SOB SOB
Phew.
!
I'M SORRY THAT I LEFT YOU...
...CHIKA-CHAN.

"CHIKA-CHAN."
WHAT...?
DID YOU KNOW...
...THE WHOLE TIME?
ストン
Oh.
IF YOU NEED HELP, TELL ME, OKAY?
YOU KNEW AND...
...HELPED "ME"?
OH.
SORRY, BUT IT LOOKED LIKE THAT YOU DIDN'T WANT ME TO KNOW.
NOW I REMEMBER THE LAST BELIEF IN THE BOOK.
AND I DON'T KNOW WHY THIS IS HAPPENING ANYWAY, SO...

MAYBE I WASN'T LOOKING AT THE TRUTH.
"BELIEVE IN FANTASY."
I WAS ALWAYS DREAMING.
THIS IS STUPID, ISN'T IT?
TOMO-CHAN.
...WHO DIDN'T REALIZE YOUR SWEETNESS.
I'M AN IDIOT...
THEN IT REALLY HAPPENED.
...IF I SWITCHED WITH SHO-CHAN AND WENT TO A BOYS' SCHOOL.
I THOUGHT THAT I COULD MEET A PRINCE...
BUT...
TO BE HONEST, I DIDN'T WANT TO BELIEVE IT.
Yeah.
I AGREE THIS IS A STUPID SITUATION.

I ALWAYS THOUGHT THAT YOU WERE CUTE...
...THE WAY YOU DREAM ABOUT THINGS AND EVERYTHING.
THAT'S WHY I KNEW IT AT ONCE.
トクン
...KIDDING ME.
YOU'RE...
トクン
トクン
WITH EVERY WORD FROM TOMO-CHAN...
I WOULDN'T SAY SOMETHING LIKE THAT AS A JOKE.

...MY HEART RANG.
トクン
かあ
トクン
トクン
トクン
OH, I SEE.
THEN, I REALIZED THAT THE SOUND WAS THE TRUTH.
I THINK...
...I'M IN LOVE WITH YOU, TOMO-CHAN.

The Door of Soul is a door for those who seek the truth.
WHEN I BECOME MYSELF AGAIN, WILL YOU GIVE ME THE ANSWER?
SLAM
CHIKA!
KNOCK
HUH...? WHY AM I IN THE BATHROOM?
KNOCK
ARE YOU ALL RIGHT, CHIKA?

I DIDN'T KNOW THAT YOU DIDN'T LIKE BOY'S LOVE COMICS.
I'M SORRY, CHIKA.
WHAT?
CREAK
RUB
RUB
Y-YEAH, I'M FINE (I THINK). WHAT'S THE MATTER?
What are you talking about?
You're crying!
WAS I DREAMING?

YOU WERE SHOCKED WHEN YOU WATCHED THE VIDEO OF A WOMAN GIVING BIRTH, WEREN'T YOU?
OR WAS IT HEALTH AND PHYSICAL EDUCATION?
I'm really sorry!
YOU GOT SICK BECAUSE I MADE YOU READ AN R-RATED ONE, RIGHT?

TOMOYAAA! WOMEN ARE SCARY!! WOMEN ARE REALLY SCARY!!!
They were there the whole time.
Every one's gay.
Then why don't you choose me? Tsk.
It's okay, it's okay...
I don't know what's going on but...
SHO--
Huh?! What?!
SHOHEI?
GASP!

How To Go Through The Secret Door / End

Heart-warming Bonus Manga

HASHIMOTO-KUN'S CONFESSION

End

Heart-warming Bonus Manga

TSUYOSHI'S FIRST PRESENT

RUSTLE
RUSTLE
SOMETHING TO MAKE SAKURA HAPPY.
Tsuyoshi's
If you touch it, I'll kill you!
Orange

ガシッ
TSUYOSHI?!
I'll give you a present when your birthday comes!

BARF ゲロッ
I'LL GIVE YOU MY TREASURES, SAKURA!
Look!
コレクション
DEAD BUGS
Cheer up. Want some cake?
I hate cake.

End ©

Heart-warming
Bonus Manga

TAKASHI'S FIRST GLASSES

The author has these glasses. End

THANKS!!

ADACHI HITOMI SAMA
MIKAMI CHITO SAMA
NAKANO EMIKO SAMA
AOI YUKI SAMA
FUJIKATA MAYU SAMA
&
KOYANO SAMA
&
KONDOU SAMA
&
YOU !!
HARI.

IN THE NEXT VOLUME OF ME & MY BROTHERS!! ♥
Cornered by Mizusawa, Sakura is in a pinch?!
DON'T MAKE ME SAY IT AGAIN.
Something happens during the summer camp?!
JUST SHUT UP AND BE MINE.
WHA--?
BRACE YOUR-SELF!!!
ME & MY BROTHERS VOLUME 5 IS COMING IN SEPTEMBER OF 2008!!!

5
4
four
three
3
2
two
1
One

TOKYOPOP®
mobile
www.TOKYOPOP.com/mobile
THE MANGA REVOLUTION • LEADING
漫画革命
THE MANGA REVOLUTION • LEADING
TOKYOPOP
Go to www.tokyopop.com/mobile
for wallpapers, ringtones and more!
www.TOKYOPOP.com

the little vampire who couldn't

Reverse vampire Karin Maaka has learned to control some of her bloodlust, but can she continue to keep it under control around Kenta, her dreamy but unhappy classmate, and negative upperclassman Ayaha Ougimachi? If Ayaha continues to incite Karin's bloodlust—well, Karin may just bite again!

anime!

POP FICTION

chibi Vampire™ The Novel

WWW.TOKYOPOP.COM

BIZENGHAST

BY M. ALICE LEGROW, NOVEL BY SHAWN THORGERSEN

Not every lost soul is a lost cause

Dinah must fight to keep her sanity and life together, *and* keep all hell from breaking loose in the Mausoleum! The town of Bizenghast holds many secrets, and Dinah will have to grow up and grow strong if she intends to seek out the truth behind the mystery.

© M. Alice LeGrow and TOKYOPOP Inc.

FOR MORE INFORMATION VISIT:

Bizenghast™

The Bizenghast Novel Debut!

When a young Dinah moves to the forgotten town of Bizenghast, she uncovers a terrifying collection of lost souls. As she is forced to help these wandering spirits, one thing becomes painfully clear: The residents of Bizenghast are just *dying* to come home. This is an unforgettable Gothic drama that will leave you haunted long after the last page is turned.

Check out the iManga at TOKYOPOP.com! Bizenghast soundtrack available on iTunes

POP FICTION

Fruits Basket™

By Natsuki Takaya

Volume 20

Can Tohru deal with the truth?

After running away from his feelings and everyone he knows, Kyo is back with the truth about his role in the death of Tohru's mother. But how will he react when Tohru says that she still loves him?

Winner of the American Anime Award for Best Manga!

The #1 selling shojo manga in America!

© 1998 Natsuki Takaya / HAKUSENSHA, Inc.

FOR MORE INFORMATION VISIT: WWW.TOKYOPOP.COM

The HILARIOUS adventures of

As Karin and Kenta's official first date continues, Anju shows up to keep an eye on the clumsy couple. When Kenta tells Karin how he really feels, will it destroy their relationship? Also, the new girl in town, Yuriya, begins snooping around in search of vampires. Why is she trying to uncover Karin's identity, and what secrets of her own is she hiding?

chibi Vampire™ Inspired the

© 2003 YUNA KAGESAKI / KADOKAWA SHOTEN

FOR MORE INFORMATION VISIT:

ABINGTON COMMUNITY LIBRARY
CLARKS SUMMIT, PA 18411

STOP!

This is the back of the book. You wouldn't want to spoil a great ending!

This book is printed "manga-style," in the authentic Japanese right-to-left format. Since none of the artwork has been flipped or altered, readers get to experience the story just as the creator intended. You've been asking for it, so TOKYOPOP® delivered: authentic, hot-off-the-press, and far more fun!

DIRECTIONS

If this is your first time reading manga-style, here's a quick guide to help you understand how it works.

It's easy... just start in the top right panel and follow the numbers. Have fun, and look for more 100% authentic manga from TOKYOPOP®!